IT TAKES A LEADER

In every community there are people who inspire others to take action.

SCHOLASTIC

LITERACY PLACE®

Copyright acknowledgments and credits appear on page 128, which constitutes an extension of this copyright page.

Copyright © 1996 by Scholastic Inc.   All rights reserved.   Printed in the U.S.A.
                                             ISBN 0-590-49191-1

          2 3 4 5 6 7 8 9 10   24   02 01 00 99 98 97 96

Over 1,200 new words!

Weber's Dictionary

3rd Edition

CHILDREN'S EXPRESS

SUKI CHEONG
EDITOR

30 Cooper Square, 4th Floor
New York, New York 10003
Tel: (212) 505-7777

IS AN AUTHORIZED REPRESENTATIVE
FOR THE CHILDREN'S EXPRESS NEWS
SERVICE. WE WILL GREATLY
APPRECIATE ANY AND ALL
COURTESIES, PASSES, AND AID THAT
YOU CAN PROVIDE.

AUTHORIZATION

Explore
a Newspaper Office

In every community there are people who inspire others to take action.

Taking Charge

People take action on issues that matter to them.

Spread the Word

People communicate on the important issues of the day.

AMERICAN RED CROSS
Radio: 30
Live Announcer Script

V.O.: Somewhere in the country...this very day...disaster struck. In fact, disaster strikes every single day. Which means every single night someone needs food, shelter, and a place to rest. You can make a difference. Please support the American Red Cross. Call 1-800-842-2200. Because every single...

Ideas in Action

It takes leadership and an organized effort to reach our goals.

Trade Books

The following books accompany this *It Takes a Leader* SourceBook.

Realistic Fiction

AWARD WINNING Author

Class President

by Johanna
Hurwitz
illustrated by
Sheila Hamanaka

Environmental Fantasy

The Great Squirrel Uprising

by Dan Elish
illustrated by
Denys Cazet

Historical Fiction

AWARD WINNING Book

Sweet Clara and the Freedom Quilt

by Deborah
Hopkinson
illustrated by
James Ransome

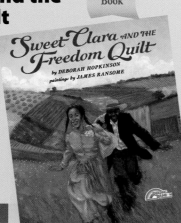

Biography

AWARD WINNING Book

Where Was Patrick Henry on the 29th of May?

by Jean Fritz
illustrated by
Margot Tomes

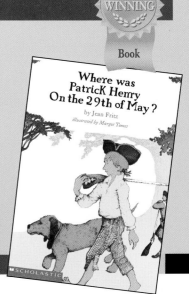

Taking Charge

Celebrate the lives of twelve African-American women as their portraits come to life.

Travel back to prehistoric times and meet Oog, a man ahead of his time. Then read about a young Native American who works for her community.

WORKSHOP 1

Take a poll and find out what people think about important issues.

School
Litter
POLL

Dinner at Aunt

by Faith Ringgold

AWARD WINNING

Book

My aunt Connie is a great artist. She and Uncle Bates live in a big beautiful house on the beach in Sag Harbor, Long Island. Every summer they invite our whole family to come for a delicious dinner and a special showing of Aunt Connie's artwork. I could hardly wait for this year's dinner—not only for the food but also for the art, which was to be a big surprise.

Connie's House

Another surprise was Lonnie, my aunt and uncle's adopted son. I fell in love with him the first time I saw him. Have you ever seen a little black boy with red hair and green eyes? Neither had I before Lonnie. While the rest of the family relaxed on the beach before dinner, Lonnie and I went in the house and played hide-and-seek.

I heard some noises up in the attic and climbed the stairs to see if Lonnie was up there.

"Come out, come out, wherever you are," I sang out.

"Come in, Melody," a strange voice answered. "We would like to talk to you."

"Lonnie, stop trying to scare me with that strange voice," I said.

I peeked into the attic and saw twelve beautiful paintings. I knew I had found Aunt Connie's surprise.

"Lonnie," I yelled, "please come out of your hiding place."

"Melody," Lonnie answered, "I am right beside you, and I heard that strange voice, too."

"Aunt Connie's paintings can talk, Lonnie."

"Paintings don't talk, Melody. Only the artist can speak."

"Yes, we can speak, Lonnie," the voice said.

"Who are you?" we chimed in chorus as we held hands and entered the strange room.

"I will be the first to speak. I am Rosa Parks. I was born in 1913 in Alabama. I am called the mother of the civil rights movement. In 1955, I was arrested for refusing to sit in the back of the bus. That incident started the Montgomery bus boycott and inspired Martin Luther King, Jr., to devote his life to the civil rights movement."

"But how can you speak? Paintings don't talk like people," Lonnie said.

"Your aunt Connie created us to tell you the history of our struggle. Would you like to hear more?"

We nodded, and the next painting spoke.

"I am Fannie Lou Hamer, born in 1917 in Mississippi. I was a civil rights activist and public speaker. I worked with Martin Luther King for voters' rights in the South. I helped thousands of people register to vote."

"My dream was education. I am Mary McLeod Bethune, born in 1875 in South Carolina. I founded Bethune-Cookman College. I was a special adviser to Presidents Franklin D. Roosevelt and Harry S. Truman and founded the National Council of Negro Women, an organization that has more than one million members."

"I was a sculptor. My name is Augusta Savage, and I was born in 1892 in Florida. I founded The Savage Studio of Arts and Crafts in Harlem. I taught many artists to paint, draw, and sculpt. Maybe you've heard of one of my students, the famous painter Jacob Lawrence?"

"My name is Dorothy Dandridge. Born in 1922 in Ohio, I was
the first African-American actress to become a Hollywood star. I
was nominated for an Academy Award in 1954 for Best Actress
for the film *Carmen Jones*. I starred in other films with famous
actors such as James Mason and Joan Fontaine."

"I am Zora Neale Hurston, born in 1901 in Florida."

"I know who you are," I said. "You're a famous writer."

"Yes, Melody. In the 1930s I was the most prolific African-American writer. My books—*Their Eyes Were Watching God*, *Moses, Man of the Mountain*, and *Mules and Men*—are considered among the best examples of American writing."

"I was born way back in 1803 in Connecticut. My name is Maria W. Stewart. Back then, women could not be public speakers, yet I spoke out for the human rights of oppressed blacks. I was also the first African American to lecture in defense of women's rights."

"I am Bessie Smith, empress of blues. I was born in 1894 in Tennessee. I was once the highest paid African-American artist in the world. The great jazz trumpeter Louis Armstrong was one of my accompanists. I inspired many singers with my soul and spirit."

"People called me Moses. I am Harriet Tubman, born in 1820 in Maryland. I brought more than three hundred slaves to freedom in the North in nineteen trips on the Underground Railroad— and never lost a passenger. Among them were my aged mother and father and my ten brothers and sisters."

"I am Sojourner Truth, born in 1797 in New York State. I was an itinerant preacher and an abolitionist with Frederick Douglass and William Lloyd Garrison. I spoke out for women's rights during slavery, when no American woman had the right to vote. I met and spoke with President Abraham Lincoln."

"I am Marian Anderson, born in 1902 in Pennsylvania. Arturo Toscanini, the great conductor, said a voice such as mine is heard only once in a hundred years. I was denied the right to sing at Constitution Hall by the Daughters of the American Revolution in Washington, D.C. In protest, I sang on the steps of the Lincoln Memorial to a crowd of 75,000. I was known as the world's greatest living contralto and was the first African American to perform with the Metropolitan Opera Company."

"Someday I want to be an opera singer, too," Lonnie said.

"My name is Madame C.J. Walker. I was born in 1867 in Louisiana. I was the first self-made American woman millionaire. I employed more than three thousand people in my cosmetics company. My invention, the hair-straightening comb, changed the appearance of millions of people."

"What do you think of us, children?" the paintings asked.

"I am very proud to be an African-American woman," I said.

"You are only a nine year old, Melody, not a woman," Lonnie said.

"And who do you think you are, Lonnie, with your red hair and green eyes? Not many African Americans look like you!"

"My hair is red and my eyes are green, but I am black, ten years old, and just as proud as you to be African American!"

Just then Uncle Bates appeared at the attic door.

"Since you two have already discovered Aunt Connie's surprise, you can help me take the paintings down to hang in the dining room."

Lonnie and I helped Uncle Bates hang the paintings on the dining room walls, then Aunt Connie called the family to dinner to see the big surprise.

Grandpa Bates was our family's toastmaster. Last year he toasted my sister Dee Dee and her fiancé, Carl's, engagement. Today he toasted Lonnie, who was Aunt Connie and Uncle Bates's son from now on. Then Lonnie read an African proverb in Swahili: "*Mti mzuri huota kwenye miiba,*" "A good tree grows among thorns." Aunt Connie's smile told us she knew we had been talking to the paintings.

Lonnie and I winked back at her, keeping the secret.

Aunt Connie's dinners are the best. We had roast turkey, duck, cranberry sauce, corn bread, stuffing, macaroni and cheese, candied sweet potatoes, and fresh greens. Seated around the table were the usual people: Aunt Connie and Uncle Bates, my mother and father, Grandma and Grandpa Bates, my sister Dee Dee and her new husband, Carl, and Mr. and Mrs. Tucker. But only Lonnie and I knew that today's dinner was extra special. It was magical. As we ate, Aunt Connie spoke about each of the women in her portraits.

Aunt Connie's paintings were no longer hanging on the dining room walls but sitting in the chairs around the table as our dinner guests. Aunt Connie's voice faded into the background, and our

family disappeared as Sojourner Truth spoke in support of the women's vote:

"Look at me . . . . I have plowed and planted and gathered into barns and no man could head me . . . I have borne thirteen children and seen most all sold into slavery, and when I cried out a mother's grief, none but Jesus heard me. And ain't I a woman?"

Harriet Tubman spoke about slavery: "There was one of two things I had a right to, liberty or death; if I could not have one, I would have the other, for no man should take me alive."

Maria Stewart spoke next, about a woman's right to speak in public. "Men of eminence have mostly risen from obscurity; nor will I, although female of a darker hue and far more obscure than they, bend my head or hang my harp upon willows, for though poor I will virtuous prove."

"Connie, your art is a great inspiration to us all," said Uncle Bates.

"Their lives speak more powerfully than any paintings could," Aunt Connie said. "Don't you think so children?" She winked her eye at Lonnie and me.

"When I grow up, I want to sing in opera houses all over the world. I know it will be hard, but not as hard for me as it was for Marian Anderson," said Lonnie.

"I want to be the president of the United States when I grow up," I said, "so I can change some of the things that make people's lives so sad. I know I can do it because of these women."

"Amen! Amen!" everybody chimed.

"I never thought my wife and the mother of our children would be the president of the United States," Lonnie whispered in my ear.

"And I never thought I would marry an African-American opera singer with red hair and green eyes," I whispered back.

"But what will our children think of Aunt Connie's secret, Melody?"

"Our children will love the secret. We will have delicious family dinners, and they will be magical just like Aunt Connie's, and our children, Lonnie, will be just like us."

from
The Big Book for Our Planet

The Last Days of the Giddywit

AWARD
WINNING
Book

by
Natalie Babbitt

illustrated by
Steven Kellogg

A Giddywit battling a fly.

Years and years ago, in the time when houses were caves—this was after the dinosaurs but a while before shovels—there was a tribe of people called the Giddywit. They lived all together, and every day the men would go out and hunt supper while the women stayed home to pick nuts and berries and teach the babies how to swat flies. Then at night, when the men came back, everyone would feast on mammoth meat or reindeer, with a side of the nuts and berries, and they tossed the garbage in a corner.

After a few weeks, of course, the pile of garbage would get pretty big and smelly, and the flies were something fierce, so the Giddywit would pack up their furs and clubs, and the babies' bibs and swatters, and move to a new cave. This always caused great confusion, with snarling and arguments, and once in a while a baby would get left behind and have to be fetched. But soon the Giddywit would be settled again in a nice fresh place and could start over, tossing garbage and swatting flies.

Now, there was among the Giddywit a thin little man named Oog who wasn't allowed to hunt mammoths because he only got in the way. So his job was to look for eggs. He was good at climbing trees, way up where the nests were, and while he was up there, he would look out over the land where everything was wild and sweet and didn't ever seem to get smelly. "This is nice," he would say to himself. "I wish *we*

could live in trees." But they couldn't because of having to hang on, even while sound asleep, which would have been hard for everyone, especially the babies. Still, Oog thought a lot about how nice it was, far away from the garbage.

One night in the cave—it was summer, and the flies and the garbage were atrocious—Oog said to everyone, "Why don't we try putting the garbage outside?"

"Outside?" said everyone. "You're a dope, Oog. If you want to bring every bear and tiger in the neighborhood nosing around the door, that's the way to do it." And they snickered at Oog and poked each other with their elbows and winked.

"We could dig holes and bury the garbage, maybe," said Oog.

"Who's got time to dig holes?" they said, with more snickers and winks. "Sure, if we had a shovel. But it's still a while before shovels. And anyway, what's wrong with moving to a new cave?"

"We might run out of caves," said Oog.

"Run out of caves!" they cried. "You're a dope, Oog." And they winked and poked each other again and threw more garbage in a corner, and then they lay down on their furs and went to sleep.

But Oog sat up, swatting flies, and thought it over. And the next morning, instead of climbing trees to look for eggs, he took Mrs. Oog by the hand and went away, a long way off, miles and miles through the wild, sweet land, and came after many days to a little cave just right for two. "This is the ticket," he said to Mrs. Oog. "We'll live on nuts and berries and the very occasional rabbit, and of course we'll always have eggs. And we'll never throw garbage into corners."

"But, dear," said Mrs. Oog, "what will we *do* with the garbage? We'll have to put it *some*where."

"We'll bury it," said Oog.

"But, dear," said Mrs. Oog, "we can't do that without shovels to dig the holes."

"We won't need very big holes," said Oog. "Not with only two. So I shall invent the spoon and dig with that."

"Clever," said Mrs. Oog. "And I shall invent the fork. To keep our fingers clean at supper. It's time."

So Oog and Mrs. Oog invented the spoon and fork and buried their garbage outside the cave, and everything stayed nice and clean, and they were happy as clams even though they'd never seen a clam, until one day, a year or so later, here came the rest of the Giddywit, tramping along with their furs and babies, arguing and snarling.

"Well, well," said Oog. "What brings the lot of you to *these* far parts?"

"We ran out of caves," said everyone. "And now you're going to snicker, aren't you?"

"No," said Oog, "but maybe you've learned that you have to bury your garbage."

"Can't do it," said everyone. "It's still too long before shovels."

"Maybe so," said Oog, "but I've invented the spoon, which is pretty good for digging."

"Oog," they said, "you're still a dope. Digging with a—what did you call it? A spoon?—is too much work for the kind of hole *we'd* need. We'll just go on and look for another bunch of caves."

So they did, still snarling and arguing, and Oog never saw them again, except, as it happens, for the babies. For the Giddywit found a new cave farther on and settled down to tossing and swatting. And then one night, when the wind was in the right direction, some bears and tigers sniffed out the cave and finished off the Giddywit, except for the babies, and left no garbage at all. The babies found their way back to Oog and Mrs. Oog, who, having no babies of their own, were delighted. And Oog made a great big spoon to dig holes with, so that shovels were invented at last, because what is a shovel but a great big spoon?

So that was the end of the Giddywit and the start of the Oogites, a neat and tidy tribe from which we are all descended.

Maybe.

from **ZuZu** JOUR

Eye on the Prize

NAL

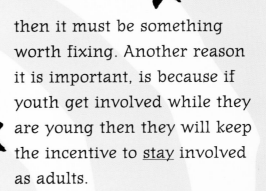

Hi, my name is Rhiannon Chavis-Legerton. I am from a small town in the southeastern part of North Carolina called Pembroke. I am a 13-year-old Lumbee Indian who has lived here all of my life. My family works in the community for justice, equality, and for correct treatment of the environment. Our organization is called the Center for Community Action.

I have been taught that youth should be involved with community work. Over time, I have grown to understand why this is so. The reason I think so is because youth have a strong say in the community. Many government officials will sometimes listen to youth more than they would adults. They figure that if the youth are strong enough to speak out

then it must be something worth fixing. Another reason it is important, is because if youth get involved while they are young then they will keep the incentive to <u>stay</u> involved as adults.

Before you can become fully involved, there will be many obstacles to overcome in the process. One of these is to ignore all of the remarks thrown at you by other people such as, "You won't win, why not just give up trying?" Over time, you will find that the only reason people say things like this is because they are really scared that you will win. Another obstacle is that if you have one teeny tiny bit of concern that you will have to work with people of other races, then get rid of it right away.

Eye on the Prize

This is because when you are fighting for something right, then it is most likely that people from other races are too. But over time, you will see that they have the same thoughts and ideas as you do.

I have done much work for change. Right now I will tell you about some of it. When I was about 5 years old, threats were made that an incinerator would be put near my home. My family and many other families worked and planned together to think of a way to stop it.

There was something for everyone to do, young and old. I have also been to Alabama to help the Choctaw stop a waste dump. I gave a speech there that was quoted on TV and in the newspaper. I am now in a multi-cultural play about a time in Robeson County when there was a lot of hatred and prejudice against people of color.

If anyone reading would like to get involved, here are some starting tips. Keep an update on the problems going on in your community. Always keep a cool head and don't blow your top every time something doesn't go your way. Go in expecting to win, and if you do, praise yourself, but don't get a big head because it might affect your attitude on the next issue. And the last tip I have is give all you can to the work and cooperate with others.

Since I have been fighting for people's rights, I have found it easier to do if you live by certain sayings.

The first one is to never give up, your luck will turn around one day.

The next one is to always look ahead, never dwell in the past or you will accomplish nothing.

The last thing that I live by is to keep your eyes on the prize, the light is never too bright.

"...Get Everyone involved including children, because if they're not they might have bad dreams or thoughts because they hear *you* talking about it. They don't understand what is happening. So... just REMEMBER - if you have them, (KIDS) INVOLVE THEM!"
— excerpt from a speech by Rhiannon (when she was 11-yrs old!)

How to
Take a Public Opinion Poll

Choose a
question
that affects
everyone.

When an organization or a town council wants to
know how a community feels about an issue, it often
takes a public opinion poll.

Give more
than one
answer.

What's a public opinion poll? A public opinion poll is the
collection of answers to questions about important issues
or events. To make the poll as accurate as possible,
different kinds of people are asked the same question.
A pollster questions both younger and
older people. The results of a public
opinion poll are often
summarized in a
bar graph.

Ask a
follow-up
question,
if it is
appropriate.

Loch Ness: Fiction Is... ...ger Than Truth

The poll should have a title.

School Litter POLL

Do you think litter is a problem at school?

If so, is it worse in the playground?

Classroom?

Are there enough trash cans provided?

Do you ever litter?

1. Decide on a Question

Choose a question on a topic that affects your classroom, school, or community. It should be a question with many possible answers; for example, how can your class work together to help your community? What charity should your school have a fundraiser for? What should your town build on the vacant lot on Main Street? After you pick your question, make up four to six possible answers.

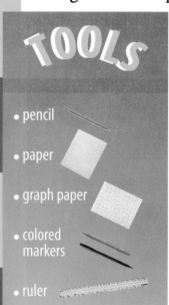

TOOLS

- pencil
- paper
- graph paper
- colored markers
- ruler

2. Create a Poll Sheet

Make a chart, and write your poll question at the top. Then put at least four possible answers to your question on the left-hand side of the page. Leave enough room between each answer so that you can fill in people's responses. Don't forget to leave a space labeled *other* to record answers you haven't thought of.

What should our town build on the vacant lot?

an in-line skating park ‖‖‖ ‖‖‖ ‖‖‖ ‖‖

tennis courts ‖‖‖ ‖

basketball courts ‖‖‖ ‖‖‖

3 Take a Poll

Ask at least ten people to answer your poll question. Try to ask a variety of people. For example, you can ask your classmates, teachers, neighbors, and family members. Record everyone's answers on your chart.

Tips
- Poll different types of people to get different opinions.
- Be polite when you ask people for their opinion.
- Mark down each answer right away so that you don't forget it.

4 Make a Bar Graph

Graph the results of your poll. Share the graph with your classmates.

Families and Free Time

In a survey, kids and their families told us how they like to spend their free time. What children like to do is represented by the red bar. What parents like them to do is shown in blue.

If You Are Using a Computer ...

This is a good opportunity to create a poll to share on-line. You can print out the answers and then create your bar graph.

THINK

Why is it important to know how others in the community feel about a certain issue?

Suki Cheong
Editor ▶

People communicate on the important issues of the day.

Spread the Word

Meet Mother Jones as she helps miners and their families stand up for their rights.

Join nine-year-old James Ale as he lobbies the mayor to build a park.

Visit Suki Cheong, an editor at *Children's Express*.

WORKSHOP 2

Pick a cause you care about and write a public service announcement.

AMERICAN RED CROSS
Radio: 30
Live Announcer Script

V.O.: Somewhere in the country...this very day...disaster struck. In fact, disaster strikes every single day. Which means every single night someone needs food, shelter, and a place to rest. You can make a difference. Please support the American Red Cross. Call 1-847-2200. Because every night is ...needs your help

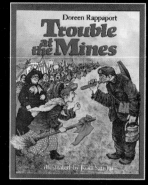
from

Trouble
at the
Mines

AWARD
WINNING

Book

by Doreen Rappaport
illustrated by Dom Lee

In 1899 the coal miners in Arnot, Pennsylvania went on strike. They hadn't had a raise in seven years and could no longer support their families. Mother Jones, a famous union organizer, promised to lead the miners and their families to victory. Ten-year-old Rosie Wilson and her cousin Mary were determined to march with Mother Jones.

OCTOBER 15, 1899

Hundreds of people were sitting in the open field outside the town waiting for the union meeting to begin. Most of them were shouting at each other.

Uncle Jack was yelling at Rosie's father. "It's four months since this strike began. Over four hundred miners have left town, and every day more are leaving. Soon there won't be any union members left. We've got to go back to work, Bryan."

"We'll never get a raise if we go back."

"Brother, if this strike continues, there's not going to be anybody left in town to use the raise."

Rosie's father grabbed his brother's forearm. "Jack, we're close to winning. All the miners in towns around are out on strike. Production is crippled. If the mine owners don't give in soon, they won't be able to get the coal for winter. We just *have* to hold out a little longer."

"Lincoln told me they've got enough coal stocked from last spring to sell through this winter. They don't need us," shouted Uncle Jack. "He also told me that if this strike continues, the mine owners are going to close the mines permanently. Then we won't need a union."

"Lincoln tells you a story, and you believe him. You're a fool, Jack." Rosie's father raised his clenched fist so near Uncle Jack's face that Rosie and Mary were sure he was going to punch him.

"You're the fool, Bryan," said Uncle Jack. He turned and marched to the front of the gathering. "Friends, friends!" he shouted. "It's been four months since the strike began. Four months ago we had a little money, and there were plenty of vegetables in the garden. Now it's almost November and we have only cabbages and sprouts left. We have no money. We can't buy food for our families. We can't pay our rent. Winter's almost here. We can't get coal to heat our houses. We have no choice but to go back to work before our families starve and freeze to death!"

Uncle Jack held up a piece of paper. "See this paper? One hundred miners, two ministers, the town doctor, the druggist, the teacher . . . signed this petition asking the owners to open the mines so we can go back to work. They've agreed. Tomorrow morning the mines will be open and anyone who wants to go back to work can. I say it's time to go back to work, before we all starve."

Rosie's mother sprang to her feet. "Don't listen to Jack," she pleaded. "If you go back now, the mine owners will never give you a raise."

Aunt Sally stood up. "I think Jack is wrong. Things will only get better if we stick together. We can't buckle under to the mine owners."

Uncle Jack hollered. "Shut up, woman. If we don't go back tomorrow, the company will shut the mines down permanently, and we won't have any jobs to go back to."

"Mine owners always threaten to close the mines down when miners ask for what they deserve!" Aunt Sally yelled back.

"What do *you* know?" Uncle Jack shouted. "You're a woman, not a miner."

Rosie's mother pointed her finger at Uncle Jack. "Scab!"

"Fool!" Uncle Jack yelled.

"Scab!"

"Fool!"

Everyone began shouting at each other. The yelling accelerated to a roar. Only Rosie's father was quiet. He scanned the crowd frantically. "Who are you looking for, Pa?" asked Rosie, pulling on his arm.

"She's come," he whispered suddenly, pointing to an old woman walking slowly across the field toward Uncle Jack.

The woman was short, with thick round glasses, a round face and a round body. Her white hair was covered by a wide-brimmed hat. She wore a long-sleeved black dress with a frilly collar.

By the time she reached Uncle Jack, the shouting had stopped. "What do you think, Mother Jones?" Rosie's father called out to her. "What should we do?"

Mother Jones clasped her hands and looked up as if in prayer. Then she looked out at the crowd, and her face broke into a slow grin. "Well," she said, "the first thing I think we should do is straighten Jack out. He's forgotten how important women are. He wouldn't be here today if it hadn't been for his mother."

Rosie and Mary looked at each other and giggled.

Amens and shrieks of laughter sounded all around them.

Her smile disappeared. "Jack has also forgotten how a miner's wife bids good-bye to her husband and sons every morning, never knowing if they'll be carried home mangled or dead. How she has to live in an overcrowded shack that's always dirty from coal dust. How she has to juggle her husband's meager wages to feed and clothe her family. And if her husband is injured, how she has to go back to work fourteen hours a day in the mills, and still cook, clean and raise the family. How can anyone believe that this strike isn't as much a woman's business as a man's?"

"Tell it to him again!" cried Aunt Sally.

"Don't she speak the truth. . . ."

"Glory be, glory be . . ."

Women called out from all directions.

"I know how hard it is for you women," Mother Jones continued, "for I too have suffered. And I know how hard it is for you men. Mining at its best is wretched work—breathing coal dust and damp air, never seeing sunlight. Never knowing when the roof might collapse, crushing your back and legs or burying you alive. Standing in sulphur water that eats through your shoes and brings sores to your flesh. Swinging your pick and ax where the roofs are so low you have to stoop over until your back aches too much to ever straighten up. A lifetime of working fourteen hours a day and nothing to show for it."

All around Rosie and Mary women were sighing and nodding their heads in agreement. Some women were crying.

Mother Jones raised her arms. "I can't argue with Jack about how bad things are. This strike has been going on for four months, and the company hasn't budged. Some of you have been thrown out of your houses. There's little or no money to buy food. No one thought it would last this long. I understand why you think going back to work is the only choice."

"Why shouldn't we?" a voice cried out.

"Because if you do," Mother Jones replied, "things will never change! Let's look at the facts. You're on strike because you're earning the same money today as you earned seven years ago. Seven years is a long time to go without a pay raise."

Her pointed finger swung in an arc around the field. "If you go back to work now, it will be for the same low wages and long hours." She lowered her voice to almost a whisper. Rosie and Mary leaned forward so as not to miss a word. "You'll die in the mines. Your sons will die in the mines and so will your grandsons. And you won't even have enough money to bury them.

"You've got to stick together. If your brothers in other mines can stay out, *you* can stay out. If they can go hungry, *you* can go

hungry. If their children can go hungry, *your* children can go hungry." Rosie squeezed Mary's hand.

Mother Jones stretched out her arms again, her voice soaring like the preacher's on Sunday. "You've got to rise and pledge to stick to your brothers until this strike is won."

Rosie's father and mother rose. Then Aunt Sally. Rosie's brother Henry stood up and began clapping and stamping his feet. Rosie and Mary jumped up and down, striking their hands together as fast and as hard as they could. One by one, other men, their wives and children by their sides, stood up. The clapping swelled until it was deafening.

Mother Jones wasn't finished yet. "At five o'clock tomorrow morning," she yelled, "I want every woman to meet me at the bottom of the hill. You men stay home and take care of the children for a change. We'll take care of any man who dares to go back to work. I want every woman to come and bring a mop, a broom, or a dishpan. Our army will make sure that no one goes into the mines." She dropped her arms and began to sing,

> "*Bring the good old bugle, boys!*
> *We'll sing another song;*
> *Sing it with a spirit*
> *That will start the world along. . . ."*

The crowd joined in, and the meeting ended in a burst of song.

Rosie's mother hugged her. "That's why mine owners call Mother Jones the most dangerous woman in America," she said.

She sure can talk, Rosie thought, but the part about the brooms and mops and the army, that was crazy.

"I must compliment you ladies." Mother Jones walked up to them. "You sure did teach those men something about courage." She took Aunt Sally's hand. "Not easy standing up like that in front of everyone, defying your husband."

"Sure wasn't," Aunt Sally said softly.

"I was stopped by the sheriff before coming to this meeting," Mother Jones continued. "He told me he had a warrant, and if I went anywhere near those mines, he'd have me arrested. Now I don't mind being arrested." She grinned. "Some of the most patriotic Americans I know have fought for justice and ended up in jail. But I don't think it would be good strategy right now to end up in jail. So one of you ladies will have to lead the army tomorrow."

"Louann had better do it," Aunt Sally said. "Jack didn't stand with the rest of us. I may have my hands full tomorrow morning with him."

"I'll gladly do it," said Rosie's mother.

"Then it's settled," Mother Jones said. "Now get your daughters home so they can get some sleep and march with us tomorrow."

October 16, 1899

It was still dark outside, but Rosie's mother was rushing around the house, banging a hammer on an old tin dishpan. "Hurry up, darlin'! Hurry up, and don't forget the broom." Rosie jumped out of bed. She dressed hurriedly, grabbed her broom and raced after her mother.

A crowd of women was gathering at the bottom of the hill that led to the mines. Rosie looked around for Mary but couldn't find her. She noticed a few of the older girls from school standing with their mothers.

Mother Jones's voice boomed as she made her way through the crowd. "How you doing? Right glad to see you. You sure look dangerous."

Rosie counted the women. Twenty. Thirty. Forty. Fifty. Six—
"Rosie!"

Rosie turned around and hugged her cousin. "Mary! Where have you been? I've been looking for you. Isn't it great? There must be at least a hundred women here. It really is like an army, isn't it?"

Mary pulled her cousin away from the crowd. "Pa left the house before anybody was up," she whispered. "He went back to work."

"I don't believe you," Rosie yelled.

"Shh! Ma told us she won't let him in the house as long as he's a scab. I never saw her so mad. Rosie, I'm scared."

"Now why are you two huddling over here?" The warmth in Mother Jones's voice surprised them. "Aren't you two girls the Wilson daughters?"

"We sure are," Rosie said proudly. Mary looked down at the ground.

"Glad to have you marching with us." She patted Mary on the shoulder. "Right good cymbal," she said, looking at Mary's dishpan. "The scabs'll sure hear you coming." She pulled out a red cloth from her dress pocket and handed it to Rosie. "Tie this to your broom. Then the scabs will see you coming."

"Mother Jones," Rosie's mother said, "I think everyone who's coming is here."

"Then let's get moving." Mother Jones turned to the crowd. "Friends, I can't go with you to the mines," she said. "I've been threatened with arrest if I do. But you don't need me. Louann Wilson will lead the army. Don't be afraid of anyone. When you see those scabs, hammer and howl. Hammer and howl. Use your mops, use your brooms and chase those men away."

Rosie's mother beat on her dishpan. "Fall in!" she cried. The women lined up behind her.

"Let's go," Rosie said to Mary, lifting her banner as high as she could.

"We will never retreat!" chanted Rosie's mother.

"We will never retreat!" cried Rosie.

"We will never retreat!" shouted Mary.

"We will never retreat." The women picked up the refrain and followed Rosie's mother along the creek and up the steep hill that led to the mines.

from
It's Our World, Too!
by Phillip Hoose

James Ale

When he was nine, James Ale saw his friend get hit by a car when they were playing ball in a crowded street. It made him wonder, Why should they have to play in the street when kids in the rich part of town had parks? The more he thought, the madder he got. Finally, James Ale took on town hall.

James Ale cried out as his friend Bobby Adams settled into position to catch the ball. Bobby was concentrating so hard that he didn't hear the white Thunderbird as it tore around the corner, heading toward him. He was on the ground, his leg bent in pain, before he even knew what happened.

James and his friends live in Davie, Florida, on the edge of the Everglades. Davie is really two towns. The western part is where rich people from Miami build ranches and keep their horses. The eastern part, where James and Bobby live, is a neighborhood of small trailers and condominiums on tiny lots.

At the time Bobby Adams was hit by the car, their neighborhood was full of children who had no place to play but in the street. At night, kids crawled around on Dumpsters left in front of construction sites. The nearest park was across a highway. You took your life in your hands every time you tried to get there. James's parents wouldn't let him even try.

As the sound of Bobby's ambulance faded into the distance, James walked slowly home. He was angry. Bobby wouldn't have gotten hurt if they had a park to play in. But officials never spent any money in this part of town.

James looked over at a small worn field right behind the water plant. That would be a perfect place for a park. There could be a playground at one end for the little kids and a basketball court at the other end. And some lights. Everyone would use it.

In that moment, James decided to make it happen. He'd organize the kids, and they'd beat down the mayor's door. They'd call themselves Children for Davie. So what if he was only nine?

That evening, James asked his dad for advice. As president of the local condominium association, John Ale was always going off to the town council meetings. If anyone would know how to pressure Davie's government, his dad would.

John Ale listened carefully to his son's idea before speaking. "You'll have to know exactly what you want and be able to prove that it's important. Playground equipment will cost money, and people ask the mayor and the town council for money every day," he said. "Everyone thinks their project is the most important thing in the world, and there's only so much tax money to go around."

Father and son sat together in silence. "But you can do it," Mr. Ale said. "More than anything, you'll have to be persistent. You can't quit."

Preparing for Action

James decided to start at the top. The next day, he telephoned the mayor.

"Mayor Kovac's office," said a pleasant voice.

"May I talk to the mayor?"

"She's not in. May I take a message?"

James left his name and telephone number. A few hours later, the mayor called him back. "I told her what had happened to Bobby Adams and said we needed a park in our neighborhood," James recalls. "I could tell she wasn't paying much attention. She seemed to be in a hurry. All she said was that she'd look into it and call me back.

"A while later she did. She said once there had been a park in our area and it had been vandalized. It was like we had blown our only chance. Then she didn't say anything. Finally I just said, 'Well, I think we need a park,' and we hung up. I felt discouraged. She treated me like a kid. I had to get her to pay attention."

James went to his room, flicked on his computer, and typed *Children for Davie* in bold print at the top of the screen. Below that, he typed out a petition calling for a new park. "Please sign this if you think that it would be better for our neighborhood if there were a park," it concluded. Beneath that he put blanks for signatures.

He printed it out, snapped it onto a clipboard, and went outside to try to get kids to sign it. They squinted at his petition, then looked at him as if he were crazy.

"Sure, man, *you're* gonna get us a park."

"Well, don't you think we need one? Look what happened to Bobby."

"Yeah, we need one, but who's gonna listen to *you*?"

"Not just me. We'll all go. She'll have to listen to all of us."

"You're outa your mind." They were starting to drift away.

"Well, just sign it if you're for it, okay?"

James got fifty kids to sign, but no one would go with him to see the mayor, not even Bobby Adams, who by now was back from the hospital and recovering from a broken leg.

James called the mayor again, this time asking for an appointment to talk about the park in person. She said yes. James prepared carefully for that meeting. Above all, he needed to be taken seriously.

Here's what he did:

- He gathered more signatures on his petition.

- He took a map of Davie and outlined the site where he wanted the park, so the mayor would know just where it should be.

- He typed out a letter on his Children for Davie stationery to leave with the mayor, listing the reasons why the park should be built and stating exactly what the town should provide: swings, a slide, monkey bars, a basketball court, and lights.

- He made up some business cards on his computer. They said, "James Ale, President, Children for Davie."

On the afternoon of the meeting, James put on his red suit jacket, a red shirt, and gray pants and squeezed into his hard black shoes. He combed his hair carefully. "When the time came for my mom to pick me up and drive me over there, I was ready."

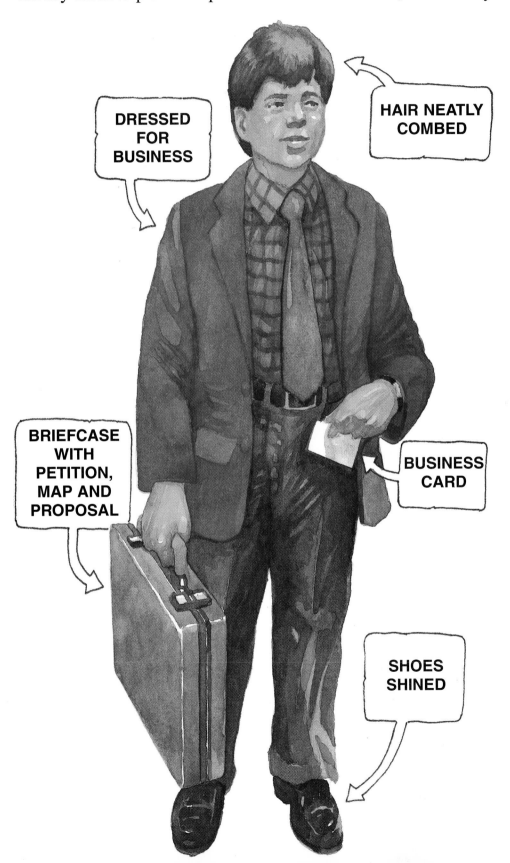

"It Should Be Here."

Mayor Joan Kovac had expected James Ale to be a child who maybe wanted to tell his friends he had met the mayor in person. But the boy who walked through the door had business on his mind. "He came in with a briefcase," she recalls. "And then he handed me a business card."

Looking directly at her, James told the mayor that his neighborhood was unsafe for kids. They had no place to play. They needed a park. It would help the town, he said, because it would save lives. The crime rate would go down because kids would have something to do. Mayor Kovac was leaning forward, looking right at him and listening carefully. When he finished, she got up and walked around her desk to a map of Davie. She pointed to three dots, clustered together on the west side of town.

"We're building three new parks right now, James," she said. "Can't your parents take you to one of them?"

CHILDREN FOR DAVIE
JAMES ALE
President 792-7758

"No," said James. "My parents both work. So do everyone else's around me. Those parks are a long way from us. We need a place of our own."

The mayor looked at the map again. "But there's no empty land where you live. Everything's all built up. Do you have a suggestion?"

James pulled the map from his briefcase and spread it on the mayor's desk. "It should be here," he said, pointing to the square he had drawn. "Behind the water plant. It's the right place. Look at this petition from the kids in the neighborhood. Everyone agrees."

Mayor Kovac had no choice but to respect him. He wasn't criticizing her or blaming the town. He had come to her with a plan. He was representing a group, and he wanted her support. She had to consider his proposal.

"Well," she said at last, "let me talk to some people in the Parks Department. We'll have to visit the site. I can't make any promises now, but I can promise I won't just put you off."

James got up and extended his hand, smiling. He pointed to his card on her desk. "My phone number is right here," he said. "I look forward to hearing from you."

"We're Going to Build That Kid a Park."

One Saturday morning a few weeks later, James met the mayor and the town administrator behind the water tower. James had been studying up on how Davie's government worked. The mayor and the town administrator were Davie's two most important officials. Along with the town attorney and the five members of the town council, they made the big decisions on how to run Davie's business. The town administrator did most of the detailed, day-to-day business.

James had gone to meet with him, too. He was a nice enough man—he had even given James tickets to a wrestling meet—but he didn't seem very interested in the park. Still, he had agreed to visit the site. Now James had the town's two most important people together right where he wanted them. This was his chance.

First James pointed to the spot where Bobby Adams had been hit. Several kids were running around. They had to agree that it would be hard for a turning car to see them.

Then James walked them around the small field. "This is the perfect place for us," James said. The administrator frowned. The lot was too small for a park, he said. He advised James to be patient. Someday the town would tear down a couple of houses and build the kids a real park.

"We don't want to wait for a bigger park," James said
flatly. "We need this park, here and now. This is the right place.
It will get used. You already own the land, and we're just
talking about playground equipment. We're not asking for
much." He could see the man's mind was closed.

If they thought James Ale would go away, they were
wrong. He waited a few days for an answer, and when none

came, he tried even harder. Nearly every day after school, he wrote brief, carefully worded letters to town officials. He also sent them updated copies of his ever-growing petition.

One night he called the secretary assigned to the town council and asked if, representing Children for Davie, he could speak briefly to the council members at Wednesday night's meeting.

"Are you a voter?" the secretary asked.

"Well, no, but I—"

"Then the answer is no," she said firmly.

James turned up the heat. He called the reporter for a Miami newspaper assigned to Davie and offered him the story of a young boy taking on town hall for the kids in his neighborhood. The reporter accepted, and a story soon appeared in the newspaper. James sent a copy to town officials.

Every few days, he called Mayor Kovac and asked her for a progress report. He was always polite. Did she need any more information? Was there anything he could do to help?

Finally his work paid off. One evening after school, James was surprised to receive a call from the town council's secretary inviting him to a council meeting. The next Wednesday evening, Mayor Kovac announced the creation of a new park. Asking him to stand, she introduced James by saying, "This boy could teach a lot of adults I know a few things about lobbying town government."

Mayor Kovac says that the small area that everyone in Davie now calls James Ale Park has become the most popular playground site in Davie. "I drive by it, and there are never fewer than thirty kids there," she says. "The parks we built in the richer parts of town are barely used. James was right."

The kids in the neighborhood thought it was a miracle that a nine-year-old boy actually got his town to spend five thousand dollars to build a park for them. But it wasn't a miracle. He simply used tried-and-true lobbying techniques.

> "This kid could teach a lot of adults I know how to lobby elected officials. He just didn't give up."
> —Mayor Joan Kovac, Davie, Florida

In Mayor Kovac's words:

- James went right to the person who had power—me, in this case—and got to know me. It was smart, because lobbying is partly personal. I like James.

- He came with a very specific plan. He had it in writing so that I could show it to people.

- His petition showed that he was representing other children.

- He was able to say, in a very few words, why that park was needed. And I could tell he really believed in it.

- He didn't come with a budget—probably he should have—but he knew what he wanted at the park. That made it easy for me to figure out the cost.

- He was always available to meet officials at the site. He provided information that we needed. He was on time.

- He was respectful. He kept pressure on us without being obnoxious or turning us off. And he listened to me.

- He was persistent. That's the most important thing of all. He just never gave up. I don't think he ever would have.

- One other thing. He paid me back, and in the right way. When my campaign for reelection came up, James called and asked if he could help. He went door-to-door asking people to vote for me. I mean he really *blitzed* that neighborhood. He was an asset to me. During the campaign, I listed the creation of James Ale Park as one of my major accomplishments.

s honore

James Ale, 12, si
Ale Park last we

Activist, 12, traveling to meet Soviet coun

By BETH DUFF SANDERS
Staff Writer

DAVIE — The road between Davie and Moscow is paved with good intentions.

And James Ale, 12, helped to lay down the asphalt.

His yearlong effort to get the town of Davie to pave over a vacant lot and build a playground for children in his small, working-class neighborhood won him national recognition and a trip to the Soviet Union.

Ale leaves today for Vermont, where he

James Ale
peace-related projects.

will join 29 other young Americans who worked to improve their communities.

On Monday, the 30 youngsters, along with adult chaperones and translators, leave for the Soviet Union on a goodwill mission sponsored by an ice-cream company known for its socially conscious and

Ale said his classmates at Driftwood Middle School in Davie "don't believe me, that I'm really going. They think I'm just pulling their leg."

But going he is.

The first stop is Moscow, then on to Kiev and Leningrad.

"And you know what? I've heard such nice things about the Russians, I don't know why we'd ever want to hurt them," Ale said on Friday, between packing and getting a haircut. "I'm going to tell them what life is like in America."

When Ale was 9 he began a relentless

string of phon
officials, dem
neighborhood
hang out on th

"I was playi
guy came aro
these hot-rod C
over," he said.

A year later,
cated at the
Terrace.

Since then, he

Rushing

g your neck out can
ut to be rewarding
s Ale, 12, saw that a
rhood a few years a
e sure one would b
received the "Stick
ctions. People who
nd the norm in com
nicknamed "giraffe

He left Saturday on
nion where he and o
are meeting with y
They are visiting Mo
about the country
Ale said they w
experiences as "

Three years a
bring a recreat
sest park for n
busy Davie Road, w
without an adult.

Instead of peste
about it, James to
of Davie.

After severa
lobbying comm
hoped to hea
Terrace had
just a shor

is
the
inor
ch as
ts and

but not
etime —
chance to

venth-grade
higher goals.
will run for
. Some people
here," Ale said.
t up."

And what did James learn? "I learned a lot. People in government will tell a kid that they don't have time for little things like a park," James says. "But if you think about it, it really is a big thing. I had a good idea and I never gave up. Kids have rights, too. But we have to learn to use them."

Suki Cheong

It's Your Brain, Not Your Color
Teenagers Discuss How Racism Affects Them

A Principal's Recipe For Racial Tolerance

Finding Solutions Without Fighting

Editor

This *editor* knows what the SCOOP is!

Since fourth grade, sixteen-year-old Suki Cheong has worked for *Children's Express,* an international news service run by kids. *Children's Express* has news bureaus in several states, and its weekly column appears in newspapers all over the country. The reporters, ages 8–13, and the editors, ages 14–18, write stories about issues such as health, education, and government. Now that Suki is an editor, she helps younger reporters get the scoop on lead stories.

PROFILE

Name: Suki Cheong

Job: student, Senior Editor/*Children's Express*

Education: Stuyvesant High School, New York City

Awards: Both a Peabody and an Emmy award for coverage of the 1988 Presidential elections

Role Model: Hillary Clinton

Favorite Newspaper Section: The Op-Ed pages

QUESTIONS
for Suki Cheong

Discover how Suki Cheong *writes about* issues from a kid's point of view.

 Q **What was your first job at *Children's Express?***

 A I started out as a reporter at *Children's Express*. Right away, I was responsible for preparing questions and doing interviews.

 Q **What's your job now that you are an editor?**

 A It's not like a typical news editor's job. I don't just edit the story—my job is to guide the reporter. I research the subject that we're doing an article on, and gather together statistics and facts we might need. If it's an interview, I set up a time and place for the interview, then brief the reporter. After an interview, I help write the actual article. I also help organize projects, conferences, and roundtable discussions.

 Q **Who chooses the stories that go into *Children's Express?***

 A Every month we have a meeting with all the kids in the bureau. We brainstorm and then vote on our ideas. Then the reporters decide which ones they want to work on.

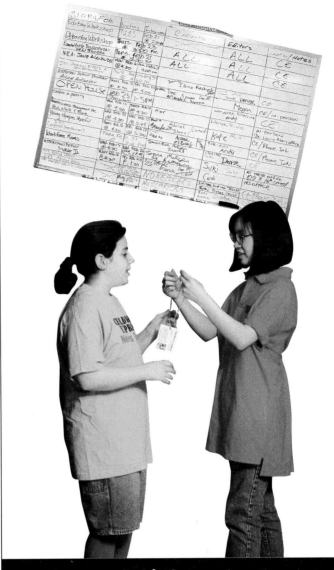

 Q **What issues do you think are important to write about?**

 A Any issues that affect children are important, such as violence in schools and on the streets, education and health. The most interesting interview I ever did was with Miguel, a sixteen-year-old who lives in a violent neighborhood. I felt it was important for people to hear his story.

 Q **Do you think that *Children's Express* can have an effect on your community and others?**

 A The purpose of *Children's Express* is to make sure that kids have a voice in their community. Maybe our stories don't always make an immediate difference. But they will make people think about an issue in a new way—from a kid's point of view.

Suki Cheong's
Tips for Young Reporters

1 Research the subject of your story or interview.

2 If it's an interview, prepare your questions ahead of time. Ask permission if you want to tape the interview.

3 Before you start writing, decide how you want to organize your story.

How to

Make a Public Service Announcement

How can you make information available to your community? One way is through a public service announcement on radio or television.

What's a public service announcement? Public service announcements give information to the community. They are broadcast free of charge by radio and TV stations. Have you ever listened to the radio and heard that your school is closed because of bad weather? That's a public service announcement! A public service announcement may also tell about a community event, such as a book fair or a fund drive.

Phone number or address for more information

AMERICAN RED CROSS •• ● **Name of the group involved**

Radio: 30

Live Announcer Script

Somewhere in the country...this very day...disaster struck. In fact, disaster strikes every single day. Which means every single night someone needs food, shelter, and a place to rest. You can make a difference. Please support the American Red Cross. Call 1-800-842-2200. Because every night is another night someone needs your help.

● **Body of message**

1 Choose a Topic

Brainstorm a list of real community issues or events for your public service announcement. Perhaps a group in your town plans to raise money for a new park, or maybe your school is putting on a play. Make a list of events and issues. Then pick the one that means the most to you.

TOOLS

- pencil and paper
- local newspapers
- posterboard and colored markers
- tape recorder (optional)

2 Organize Your Facts

Do research to learn more about the issue or event you chose. You can read the local newspaper, watch the local TV news, or talk to people in your community. Take notes on what you learn. When you're finished, see whether you can answer the "5 Ws": Who, What, When, Where, and Why. If you can't, you'll need to do some more research.

Support THE In-line Skating Park

3 Write a Script

Here's how to write a script for your public service announcement.

- Say that you are making a public service announcement.
- Tell the name of the group that is involved.
- State the reason for the announcement.
- If you are announcing an event, give the time and place that it will be held.
- Explain to the audience members how they can get more information.
- Try to use words that will catch your audience's attention.

Tips
- State your message in the fewest words possible.
- Use action verbs to make your announcement more interesting.
- Listen to radio and TV announcers to see how they sound.
- Practice saying your announcement before you present it.

4 Present Your Public Service Announcement

There are many ways to present your public service announcement. You can read it "live" to the class, or read it into a tape recorder and play the tape for the class. You might want to add music and sound effects to make the announcement more dramatic.

If You Are Using a Computer . . .

Use the Record and Playback tools as you write your public service announcement on the computer. You also may want to create a public service announcement, using clip art and borders, to appear in a newspaper.

THINK

Why are public service announcements an important service for the community?

Suki Cheong
Editor ▶

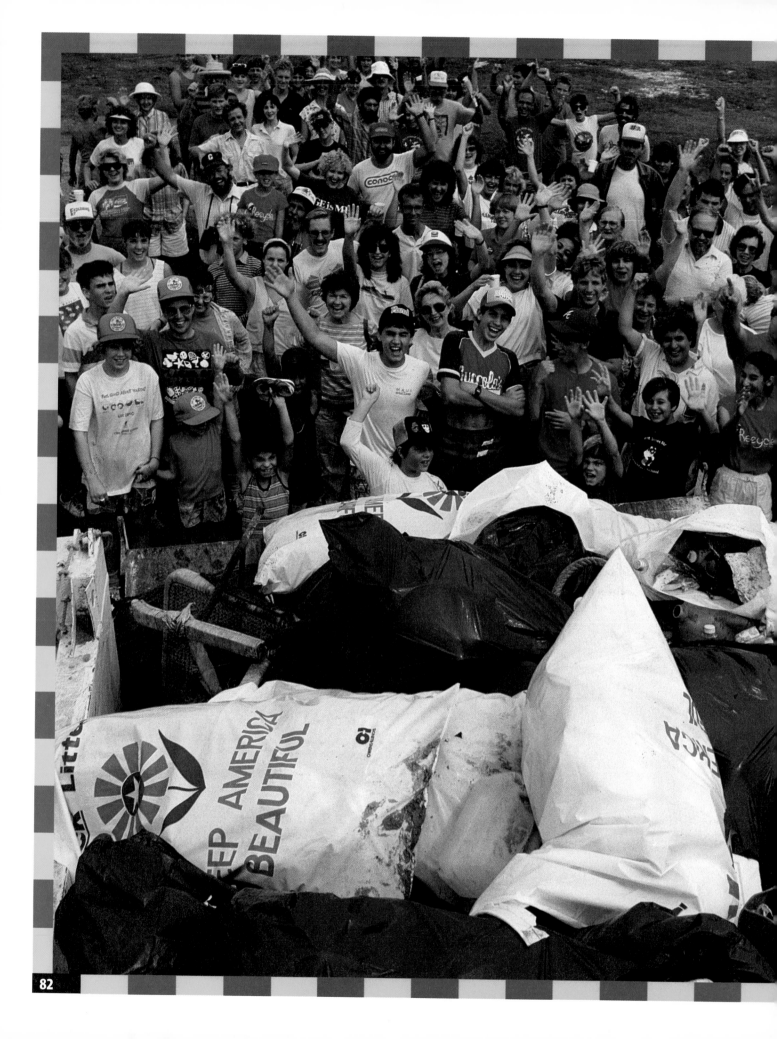

It takes leadership and an organized effort to reach our goals.

Ideas in Action

Find out how Jackie Robinson became the first African American to play major league baseball.

Follow a father and son on their mission to save Mexico's last rain forest. Then read letters from kids in China who want to help save the environment.

PROJECT

Make your opinion known— write a letter to the editor.

Teammates

AWARD
WINNING

Book

Jackie Robinson

"Pee Wee" Reese

by **Peter Golenbock**
Illustrated by **Paul Bacon**

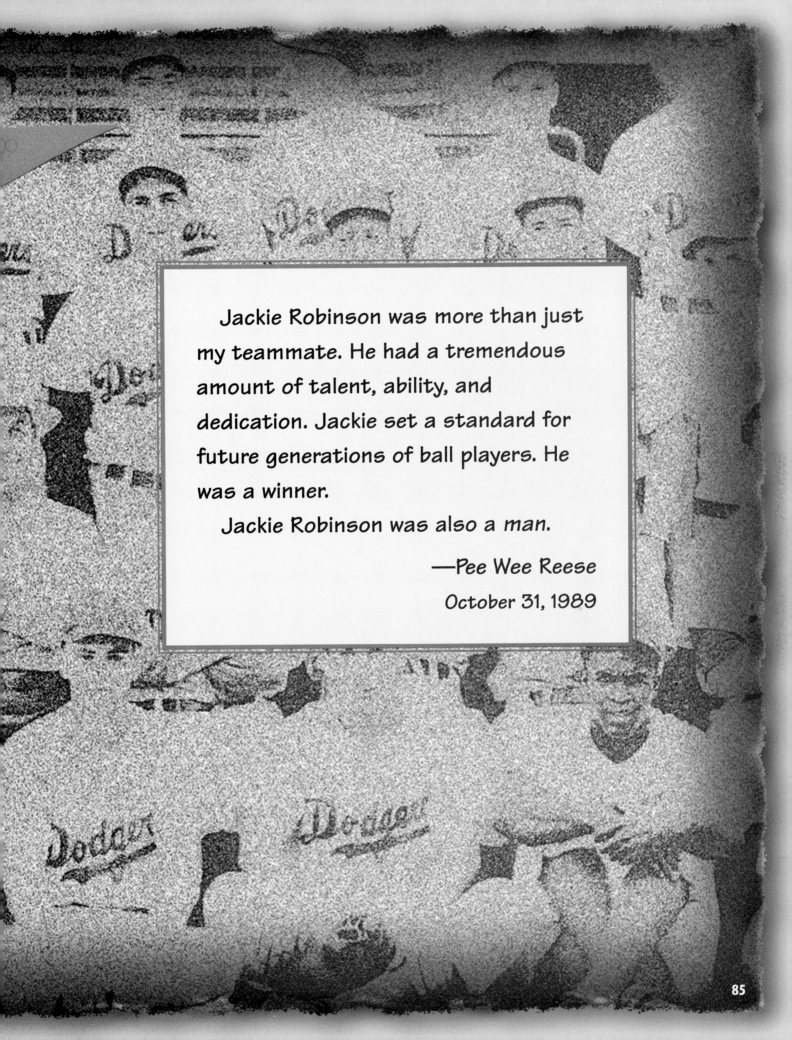

Jackie Robinson was more than just my teammate. He had a tremendous amount of talent, ability, and dedication. Jackie set a standard for future generations of ball players. He was a winner.

Jackie Robinson was also a *man*.

—Pee Wee Reese

October 31, 1989

SATCHEL PAIGE

Once upon a time in America, when automobiles were black and looked like tanks and laundry was white and hung on clotheslines to dry, there were two wonderful baseball leagues that no longer exist. They were called the Negro Leagues.

The Negro Leagues had extraordinary players, and adoring fans came to see them wherever they played. They were heroes, but players in the Negro Leagues didn't make much money and their lives on the road were hard.

Laws against segregation didn't exist in the 1940s. In many places in this country, black people were not allowed to go to the same schools and churches as white people. They couldn't sit in the front of a bus or trolley car. They couldn't drink from the same drinking fountains that white people drank from.

Back then, many hotels didn't rent rooms to black people, so the Negro League players slept in their cars. Many towns had no restaurants that would serve them, so they often had to eat meals that they could buy and carry with them.

"JOE" DI MAGGIO

SPORT KINGS GUM

TY COBB

LOU GEHR.

Lou Gehrig— says..

Life was very different for the players in the Major Leagues. They were the leagues for white players. Compared to the Negro League players, white players were very well paid. They stayed in good hotels and ate in fine restaurants. Their pictures were put on baseball cards and the best players became famous all over the world.

Many Americans knew that racial prejudice was wrong, but few dared to challenge openly the way things were. And many people were apathetic about racial problems. Some feared that it could be dangerous to object. Vigilante groups, like the Ku Klux Klan, reacted violently against those who tried to change the way blacks were treated.

The general manager of the Brooklyn Dodgers baseball team was a man by the name of Branch Rickey. He was not afraid of change. He wanted to treat the Dodger fans to the best players he could find, regardless of the color of their skin. He thought segregation was

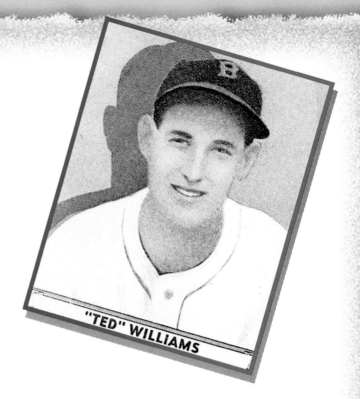

unfair and wanted to give everyone, regardless of race or creed, an opportunity to compete equally on ballfields across America.

To do this, the Dodgers needed one special man.

Branch Rickey launched a search for him. He was looking for a star player in the Negro Leagues who would be able to compete successfully despite threats on his life or attempts to injure him. He would have to possess the self-control not to fight back when opposing players tried to intimidate or hurt him. If this man disgraced himself on the field, Rickey knew, his opponents would use it as an excuse to keep blacks out of Major League baseball for many more years.

Rickey thought Jackie Robinson might be just the man.

Jackie rode the train to Brooklyn to meet Mr. Rickey. When Mr. Rickey told him, "I want a man with the courage not to fight back," Jackie Robinson replied, "If you take this gamble, I will do my best to perform." They shook hands. Branch Rickey and Jackie Robinson were starting on what would be known in history as "the great experiment."

At spring training with the Dodgers, Jackie was mobbed by blacks, young and old, as if he were a savior. He was the first black player to try out for a Major League team. If he succeeded, they knew, others would follow.

Initially, life with the Dodgers was for Jackie a series of humiliations. The players on his team who came from the South, men who had been taught to avoid black people since childhood, moved to another table whenever he sat down next to them. Many opposing players were cruel to him, calling him nasty names from their dugouts. A few tried to hurt him with their spiked shoes. Pitchers aimed at his head. And he received threats on his life, both from individuals and from organizations like the Ku Klux Klan.

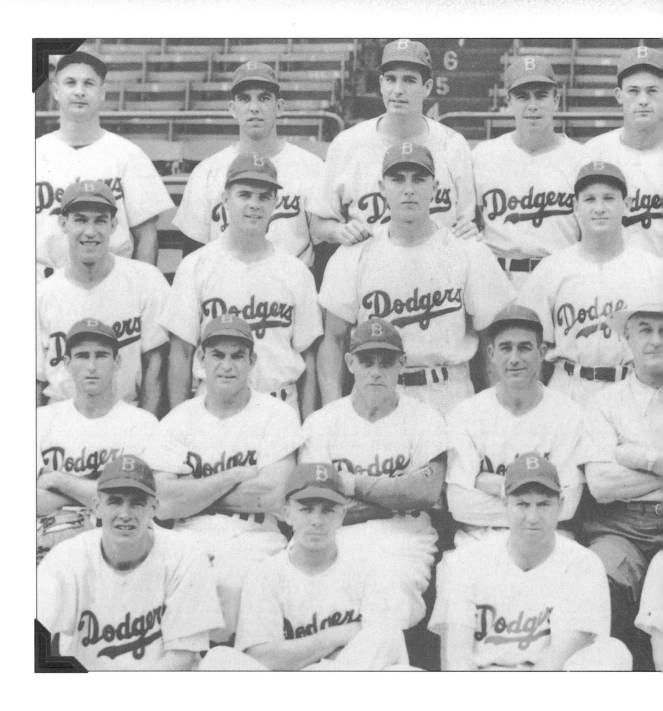

Despite all the difficulties, Jackie Robinson didn't give up. He made the Brooklyn Dodgers team.

But making the Dodgers was only the beginning. Jackie had to face abuse and hostility throughout the season, from

April through September. His worst pain was inside. Often he felt very alone. On the road he had to live by himself, because only the white players were allowed in the hotels in towns where the team played.

The whole time Pee Wee Reese, the Dodger shortstop, was growing up in Louisville, Kentucky, he had rarely even seen a black person, unless it was in the back of a bus. Most of his friends and relatives hated the idea of his playing on the same field as a black man. In addition, Pee Wee Reese had more to lose than the other players when Jackie joined the team.

Jackie had been a shortstop, and everyone thought that Jackie would take Pee Wee's job. Lesser men might have felt anger toward Jackie, but Pee Wee was different. He told himself, "If he's good enough to take my job, he deserves it."

When his Southern teammates circulated a petition to throw Jackie off the team and asked him to sign it, Pee Wee responded, "I don't care if this man is black, blue, or striped"— and refused to sign. "He can play and he can help us win," he told the others. "That's what counts."

CROSLEY FIELD

Very early in the season, the Dodgers traveled west to Ohio to play the Cincinnati Reds. Cincinnati is near Pee Wee's hometown of Louisville.

The Reds played in a small ballpark where the fans sat close to the field. The players could almost feel the breath of the fans on the backs of their necks. Many who came that day screamed terrible, hateful things at Jackie when the Dodgers were on the field.

More than anything else, Pee Wee Reese believed in doing what was right. When he heard the fans yelling at Jackie, Pee Wee decided to take a stand.

With his head high, Pee Wee walked directly from his shortstop position to where Jackie was playing first base. The taunts and shouting of the fans were ringing in Pee Wee's ears. It saddened him, because he knew it could have been his friends and neighbors. Pee Wee's legs felt heavy, but he knew what he had to do.

As he walked toward Jackie wearing the gray Dodger uniform, he looked into his teammate's bold, pained eyes. The first baseman had done nothing to

provoke the hostility except that he sought to be treated as an equal. Jackie was grim with anger. Pee Wee smiled broadly as he reached Jackie. Jackie smiled back.

Stopping beside Jackie, Pee Wee put his arm around Jackie's shoulders. An audible gasp rose up from the crowd when they saw what Pee Wee had done. Then there was silence.

Outlined on a sea of green grass stood these two great athletes, one black, one white, both wearing the same team uniform.

"I am standing by him," Pee Wee Reese said to the world. "This man is my teammate."

from

Save My Rainforest

by Monica Zak
illustrated by Bengt-Arne Runnerström
English version by Nancy Schimmel

Omar Castillo lives in Mexico City. His grandfather has told him about the last rainforest in Mexico, and Omar dreams of visiting it someday. One evening while watching the news on TV, Omar learns about the destruction of the rainforest. He convinces his father that they must take action. They decide to walk to save the rainforest.

Early one morning Omar and his father start walking. At first Omar is smiling and singing. On the road at last! And tonight, for the first time in his life, he will sleep in a tent.

For hours and hours they walk on the hot pavement. Finally, they leave the dirty yellow air of the city for the clear, clean air of the countryside. But Omar is too tired to notice. Then his feet begin to hurt. He goes a good ways before he says anything. When he does, his father stops and takes Omar's shoes off. "You have blisters. I'll put a bandage on . . . there. Now we can get started again."

"But Papa, I'm too tired. I can't go on."

"I'm tired too," says his father, "but try to go a little farther. I'll buy us a cool drink at the next store." They find a fruit stand where a woman with long braids sells them tall glasses of pineapple drink.

She looks at them curiously and finally asks, "What does your banner say? I can't read."

Omar revives at once. "This side says 'Let's protect the rainforest' and the other side says 'Walk—Mexico City—Tuxtla Gutiérrez.' Tuxtla's a long way south of here, but that's where we decided to go, to see the governor of the state of Chiapas, where the rainforest is. He is responsible for taking care of it. We need to tell him to save the rainforest so there will still be a rainforest in Mexico for us children when we grow up."

"You must be sent from heaven!" she says.

Omar's father smiles. "No, he's just a regular kid. All kids have good ideas, but usually people don't listen to them. It never made any difference to me that they were destroying the rainforest and the animals, but when I thought about what my son said, I realized that he knew what he was talking about. That's why I decided to come with him."

Another day, the sun beats down through the thin mountain air. This time it is Omar's father who has blisters. He calls, "Must you walk so fast, Omar?"

After walking more than a week, they come down out of the mountains. They can see banana plantations now, and *mango* trees. They camp by the side of the road.

Omar lies in the tent and listens. The night before, he heard coyotes howling near the tent: ah-ooo, ah-ooo, ah-ooo. He was afraid. Now he listens to the murmuring leaves. *What if a snake should get into the tent? What if robbers attack us?* he thinks. An enormous truck rumbles past and shakes the tent. *What if the driver fell asleep and . . .*

"Omar, are you awake?" his father asks.

"Mm-hm," answers Omar. "I can't sleep."

"Well," says Omar's father, "we really had a tough day. Heat, no shade, and traffic. Now it's pleasant. We won't be cold tonight."

"No," says Omar, smiling. "Remember the first night in the tent? I thought it would be wonderful, camping, but then the rain started . . ."

"Yes," says his father, "and the water came in. At three in the morning! Remember how good that hot *pozole* tasted after we walked in the dark and cold?"

"Papa, how many more days do we have to walk?"

"I thought it would take fifteen or twenty days, but it will take much longer. I don't want to disappoint you, but I don't believe we can go on."

"But why?" asks Omar, astounded.

"We are running out of money."

They decide to keep going.

"We will have to beg for food," says Omar.

They go into a restaurant and Omar's father explains to the owner why they are walking. "We have no more money," Omar's father says, "and my son is awfully hungry." The owner turns them out without giving them even a glass of water. But then a woman sitting outside a little hut motions them in, makes a fresh pot of coffee, and serves them coffee and bread. It goes like that. Some days people give them food, but often they have to walk the whole day without eating anything. Those days are hard.

When Omar sees boys playing soccer, he stops and watches with envy, but they never ask him to play. Sometimes there are things to look at in the road: a huge scorpion or snakes run over by cars. But more often, walking is boring. Omar throws rocks at fenceposts, thinking *Why didn't I bring anything to play with?* Then somebody who hears he is going to the rainforest gives him a toy Tarzan. He passes the time pretending Tarzan is in the rainforest, swinging from vines.

People warn them not to take the shortest way to Tuxtla, the road that goes through poor villages. "They'll attack you and rob you. It's too dangerous!" But Omar and his father take that road anyway, because it is 125 miles shorter. At first they are a little afraid, but no one attacks them. In fact, women and children come out and give them oranges and *tortilla* chips.

On the morning of their twenty-fifth day of traveling, Omar's father wakes him with "Las Mananitas" on his harmonica. Omar had forgotten—today he is nine! His father gives him a big hug and kiss, but Omar can see that he is sad—there is no money for birthday presents. Then, in the afternoon, they come to a little village where the people have already heard about their walk to save the rainforest. When they find out it is Omar's birthday, a woman bakes him a cake and invites all the neighbors for a real *fiesta de cumpleaños.* The house is full of people. And the cake! It is enormous, and chocolate, and has nine candles.

Everyone says, "Omar, blow out the candles!" What a lucky day! Omar grins whipped cream and chocolate from ear to ear.

A few days later they stop in a little town to eat in a restaurant. An announcer comes on television to say there has been a terrible earthquake in Mexico City.

They see a picture of a big pile of rubble and hear that it is the hospital where Omar's grandmother works! Omar starts to cry. His father has tears in his eyes. No one can reach Mexico City by telephone

because the lines are out. Then a ham radio operator in the town promises he will help them get news.

After four days of waiting, the radio operator says, "Your *abuela* is alive, Omar. She wasn't in the hospital when the earthquake came. Your mother is well. She sends you kisses and says your house wasn't hurt at all. She wishes you a safe journey."

And now they can continue.

After thirty-nine days of walking, Omar and his father come to Tuxtla Gutiérrez. They have travelled 870 miles and they are tired. They have to wait the whole day outside the governor's office, but finally the moment comes that Omar has been hoping for.

His heart beats loudly as he faces the governor and says, "Save my rainforest and stop the hunting of the rainforest animals for the next twenty years." The governor pats Omar on the head and says there is nothing to worry about.

Omar still worries. *He is treating me like a kid,* he thinks. *He won't do anything.*

But Omar does get to see a rainforest. When Tuxtla was built, a piece of the rainforest was left as a park. At first, Omar is disappointed in the rainforest, too. There aren't lots of strange animals running around in plain sight. Just gigantic trees and a clean wet smell.

Omar stands quietly for a long time in the deep green light amid the huge trunks, listening to all the birds singing high above in the canopy of leaves. Then he knows that being in a real rainforest at last is worth the trouble of walking 870 miles.

Omar and his father meet the zoologist, Don Miguel, who takes care of the park. Don Miguel explains, "They cut some of the trees for lumber, but mostly they are cutting the forest, and even burning some of the trees, to clear land to graze cattle. Every time somebody eats a hamburger, the people who cut the rainforest get more money.

"You saw how dry the land is around Tuxtla. It's dry because the rainforest is gone. Cutting down the forest changes the climate. Now this little piece of rainforest has to be irrigated to preserve it. It's a rainforest without rain!"

Omar also learns that medicines come from the rainforest plants. More medicines could be found if the rainforests were left standing.

"I am old and tired," says Don Miguel to Omar's father. "I have been fighting all my life to save the rainforest. I don't have the strength to go on. So I am happy to know there are people like this boy. It gives me hope."

When Omar hears Don Miguel say this, he knows he can't give up. *I have to talk to the President,* he thinks. *After all, he is the one responsible for the whole country.*

When they get home, Omar goes to see the President. But it doesn't matter that he walked all the way to Tuxtla Gutiérrez to save the rainforest. The President will not see him.

So Omar and his father set up the little red tent under the President's balcony. Immediately a crowd gathers.

"Are you crazy?" they ask. "Why are you camping in the *Zocalo*?"

"Because I want to talk to the President," explains Omar, "and I won't leave until he listens to what I have to say."

All the cold December day, he marches around the huge plaza with his banner. By night, Omar's teeth are chattering, and still the President has not come out.

The next day, the newspapers run a story about Omar. More people come to see him.

Drivers give him the thumbs-up sign or call out to him, "*Arriba*, Omar! We're with you! Save the rainforest!"

That night, people Omar and his father don't even know come to guard them as they sleep.

Children come to play with Omar. They listen to the story of his walk. They make paper signs and start parading about the *Zocalo* with him.

"We will save the rainforest!" they shout at the top of their lungs. For four days.

Finally, Omar is so tired that he stops under the President's balcony and yells, "Señor Presidente! I am hungry and cold. Please let me come in. Señor Presidente, if you have children, think about them." No one appears on the balcony. Omar starts walking again. Two hundred times around the *Zocalo*. Then a man comes to tell Omar that the President wants to talk to him.

"Papa! It's happened!" shouts Omar, running to give his father a big hug. The children cheer as Omar goes into the palace. He knows he doesn't have much time so he just says the most important thing. He asks the President to save the last great rainforest of the country so it can be left to the children of Mexico as their inheritance.

The President promises Omar that in one year, the rainforest cutting will stop and nobody will be allowed to capture the rainforest birds and animals to sell them for pets.

Omar comes out of the presidential palace walking on air.

For a while, Omar is content, thinking that the President will save the rainforest.

A year later Omar goes to the Sonora Market in the center of the city. He looks at the beautiful toys, but he is really there to see the animals. In the corner of the huge marketplace where they sell pets, he finds a *toucan* in a cage.

The President had promised that no more rainforest creatures would be caught and sold, but he has broken his promise. Omar knows they are still cutting down trees, too. "I promise to keep working to save your home," Omar says to the *toucan*, "and I will keep *my* promise."

GLOSSARY

abuela—grandmother

arriba—hurray

fiesta de cumpleaños—birthday party

mango—tropical fruit

pozole—hominy soup

tortillas—corn or wheat flat bread

toucan—tropical bird

Zocalo—main square or plaza

The 870-mile route that Omar and his father walked

Did you enjoy this story of the boy who wanted to save the rainforest? Well, it isn't a story. I am Omar Castillo. Now I am eleven; all that you read in this book happened when I was eight and nine.

I was very young then. I thought I had to do everything myself. I thought it would be enough to go and talk to the grown-ups who have the power to make decisions. I thought it would be enough just to say "Save my rainforest." Now I know this is not the way it works.

When I saw that they would keep destroying the rainforest, I went by bicycle to various states of Mexico. I asked the governors to write to the President asking him to protect the forests, but few of them agreed.

This showed me that I will not be able to save the rainforest by myself. It will take many of us to do that.

Now I have talked to many children in Mexico and I know that they think as I do: all children want a rainforest to be there when we grow up. And all the children I have talked to are as determined as I am. If the grown-ups don't stop cutting the Lacandon Rainforest, we will all have to go there; hundreds of thousands of children will make a chain that will surround the rainforest. And we will not move until they stop logging!

SOURCE

Dear World
How Children Around the World
Feel About Our Environment

EDITED BY LANNIS TEMPLE

Letters

AWARD
WINNING

Book

from

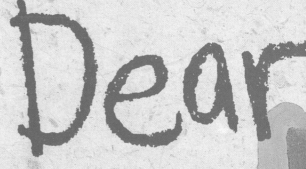

How Children Around the World Feel About Our Environment

edited by *Lannis Temple*

Dear World,

When I have time, I go into the forest and sit under a big tree. Then if I sit there for several hours without moving, without speaking, the animals start to come out. After a while, they're not afraid of me. Perhaps they think I'm a rock. If I'm very patient, sometimes small animals come right up to me. When that happens, I feel very happy because I know nature won't hurt me. Nature is like my second mother, whenever I need her she will help me.

But now many people are starting to go into the forest. They camp there, eat there, but when they go they leave all their rubbish behind them. Very unhealthy! How can they be so thoughtless? After they've left, the animals come back. They might eat a cardboard box, a plastic bag and then that bag might stick in their throat, so they can't get rid of it. Then they'd die. Really terrible!

I hope people will wake up. I want to tell the people of the world if they don't hurry up and protect nature, in a few years there won't be any nature.

Your friend,

Pu Lan

Age 13

你的朋友： 浦兰

13岁

World

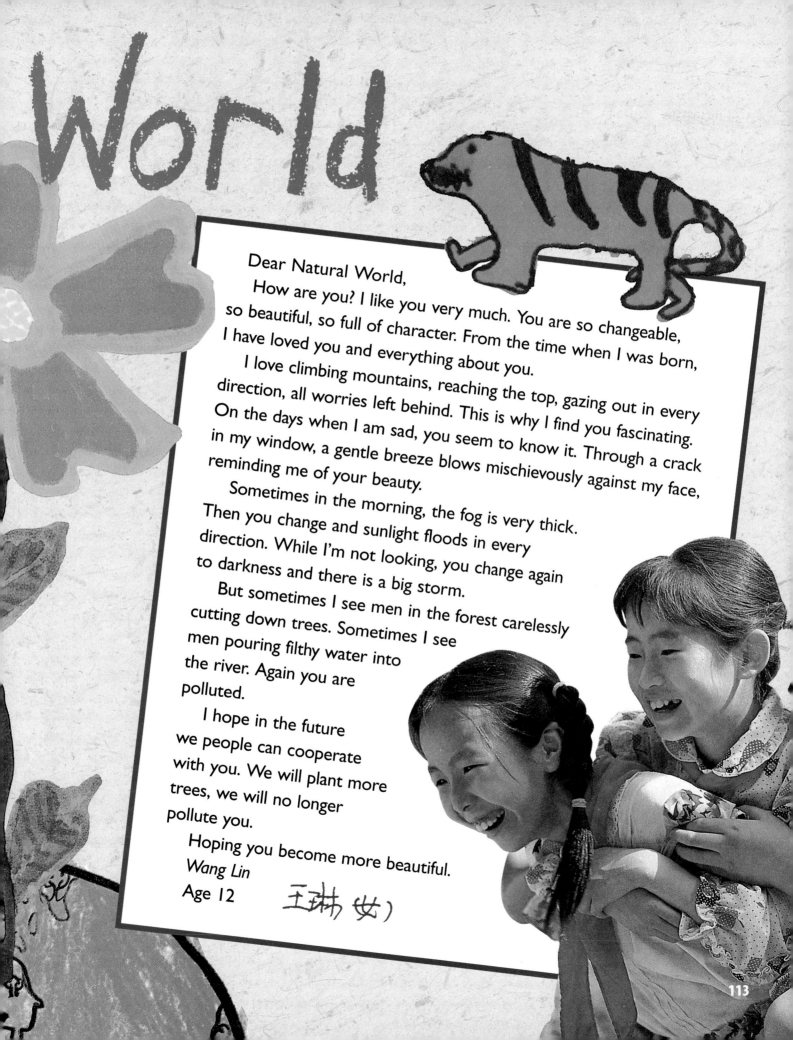

Dear Natural World,

How are you? I like you very much. You are so changeable, so beautiful, so full of character. From the time when I was born, I have loved you and everything about you.

I love climbing mountains, reaching the top, gazing out in every direction, all worries left behind. This is why I find you fascinating.

On the days when I am sad, you seem to know it. Through a crack in my window, a gentle breeze blows mischievously against my face, reminding me of your beauty.

Sometimes in the morning, the fog is very thick. Then you change and sunlight floods in every direction. While I'm not looking, you change again to darkness and there is a big storm.

But sometimes I see men in the forest carelessly cutting down trees. Sometimes I see men pouring filthy water into the river. Again you are polluted.

I hope in the future we people can cooperate with you. We will plant more trees, we will no longer pollute you.

Hoping you become more beautiful.

Wang Lin

Age 12

王琳 女）

113

How to

Create an Op-Ed Page

State *your* opinion in a letter to the *editor*.

Many newspapers have an Op-Ed page. Editorials and letters to the editor appear on this page. Editorials are articles in which the newspaper's editors give their opinions. The letters are from readers, giving their opinions. Many different kinds of issues are discussed on the Op-Ed page.

Temple edge

Will meet UMass in Atlantic 1...

The P...

New Jersey Edition

Concerns deepen about the dollar

The decline against other currencies continues. "Everyone seems to want currencies other than the dollar," one observer s...

By Andrew Cass...
INQUIRER STAFF WR...

The Mexican bailout... fiscal year. A waveri... All were being... for the stomach. A... dollar, a plunge tha... of inflation, recession liv... squeeze on American liv... ards.

The dollar fell to a record... 92.59 yen in late afternoon tra... New York, down from Frida... 93.70. It also declined ag... German mark, droppin... marks... level... than...

OP-ED DEPT

The letter arrives at the Op-Ed Department.

INCOMING LETTERS

EDITOR

The letter is read by an editor.

Once approved, it goes to the fact checker who verifies the information in the letter.

FACT CHECKER

PROOF READER

The letter then goes back to the Op-Ed Department, where it is edited for publication.

1 Explore Your Options

Think about a list of topics for a letter to the editor. Focus on issues that are important in your school or community, and choose the one you care about the most. Research the topic by reading community newspapers, talking to people, and listening to the local news. Take notes as you do your research. Decide what your opinion is about the issue.

TOOLS

- paper and pen
- local newspapers
- envelope and stamp

Recycling

Tips • If you want, work with a classmate to gather information about an issue. You take one side of the issue, and your friend takes the other.

• Interview people and write down their opinions. Be sure to get their names.

• Call or write to community leaders and see how they feel about the issue.

2 Organize Your Information

Once you have researched the issue you want to write about, it's time to outline your letter. The first part of your letter will introduce the issue. The second part will give facts and maybe some quotes about the issue.

Your last paragraph will state your opinion on the issue and any suggestions you might have. Make notes about what you will include in each part of your letter.

How Am I Doing?

Before you write your letter to the editor, take a few minutes to ask yourself these questions.

- Did I pick an issue that's important to my community?

- Did I gather facts and examples to support my opinion?

- Did I make an outline to organize my material?

Write Your Letter to the Editor

On the right side of a piece of paper, write your address and the date. On the left side, write the newspaper's address. (You can find this information inside the newspaper.) Then write *Dear Editor,* and begin your letter. Use persuasive writing to get your point across, and support your opinions with facts and quotes. End with *Yours truly* or *Sincerely.* Sign your letter in script, and print your name underneath. Use this letter to create a class Op-Ed page. Mail a copy of your letter to the local newspaper, too. Be sure to put a stamp on the envelope!

Editor
Op-Ed Dept.
Newspaper Times
1112 Print Rd.
Typee, TN 40432

24 Seal Dr.
Oakridge, TN 43044
3/13/95

To Editor:
I am writing to
express m

Jane Smith
24 Seal Drive
Oakridge, TN 43044

Op-Ed Departmen
Newspaper Times
1112 Print Rd.
Typee, TN 40432

4 Assemble the Op-Ed Page

Gather all the letters in the class to create a big Op-Ed page. You may wish to use mural paper or a posterboard as the base. Work together to arrange the letters. Make up a name for your class newspaper, and then add the date. Display the Op-Ed page on a school bulletin board so that everyone can read it.

If You Are Using a Computer ...

Write your letter on the computer in the letter format. Choose a letterhead and create your own personal stationery. You also may want to create a headline banner for your Op-Ed page, using a large special font.

THE OPINION BOARD

CONGRATULATIONS You have learned that it's possible to create change. Remember to use the skills you've learned to help you take a stand on important issues.

Suki Cheong
Editor ▶

Glossary

ab•o•li•tion•ist
(ab ə lish′ə nist) *noun*
A person who worked to abolish slavery. Frederick Douglass was a famous *abolitionist*.

ac•com•plish
(ə kom′plish) *verb*
To complete; achieve.

ac•tiv•ist
(ak′tə vist) *noun*
A person who takes action to help the community.

ap•a•thet•ic
(ap′ə thet′ik) *adjective*
Having little interest; indifferent.

boy•cott
(boi′kot) *noun*
A planned refusal to have anything to do with a person, group, or nation. They organized a *boycott* of imported products.

Word History

Boycott comes from a person's name. In 1897 an English landlord named Charles Boycott refused to lower rents on his property in Ireland. The tenants responded by paying him no rent at all.

civ•il rights
(siv′əl rīts) *noun*
The rights of personal liberty guaranteed to U.S. citizens by the Constitution and acts of Congress.

com•mu•ni•ty
(kə myōō′ni tē) *noun*
All the people who live together in one area.

coun•cil meet•ings
(koun′sel mēt′ ings) *noun*
Gatherings of city or county government officials to make laws.
▲ **council meeting**

hos•til•i•ty
(ho stil′i tē) *noun*
Resistance; conflict; ill will. She felt the soldier's *hostility*.

hu•mil•i•a•tions
(hyōō mil′ ē ā′shənz) *noun*
Offensive, insulting acts. The hero suffered many *humiliations* before he reached his goal.
▲ **humiliation**

Word History

The word **humiliations** comes from the Latin word *humiliatus* which means "to humble."

ir·ri·gat·ed
(ir′i gā tid) *verb*
Brought water to dry
land to help crops grow.
We *irrigated* the fields in
the summer. ▲ **irrigate**

irrigated

lob·by·ing
(lob′ē ing) *verb*
Trying to convince
lawmakers to vote a
certain way. They were
lobbying the town coun-
cil to build a park.
▲ **lobby**

log·ging (lo′ging) *verb*
Cutting trees for lumber.
▲ **log**

logging

march·ing
(mâr′ching) *verb*
Moving forward in a
steady way, in step with
others. ▲ **march**

marching

a	add	o͝o	took	ə =
ā	ace	o͞o	pool	a in *above*
â	care	u	up	e in *sicken*
ä	palm	û	burn	i in *possible*
e	end	yo͞o	fuse	o in *melon*
ē	equal	oi	oil	u in *circus*
i	it	ou	pout	
ī	ice	ng	ring	
o	odd	th	thin	
ō	open	th	this	
ô	order	zh	vision	

meet·ing
(mē′ting) *noun*
A coming together of two or more people for a common purpose.

news·pa·per
(nōōz′pā′pər) *noun*
A printed paper published daily or weekly that contains news.

op·pos·ing
(ə pō′zing) *verb*
Being against something; resisting. The town was *opposing* the construction of a new highway.
▲ **oppose**

op·pressed
(ə prest′) *adjective*
Persecuted; governed unjustly. The people felt *oppressed* by the new laws.

or·gan·i·za·tion
(ôr′gə nə zā′shən) *noun*
A group of people who work together for a particular purpose.

o·ver·come
(ō vər kum′) *verb*
To get the better of someone or something.

pe·ti·tion
(pə tish′ən) *noun*
A formal written request usually signed by those who support it.

plan (plan) *noun*
A method or way of doing something that has been thought out beforehand.

Thesaurus
plan
proposal
project
design

plan·ta·tions
(plan tā′shənz) *noun*
Estates in tropical regions that grow cultivated crops.
▲ **plantation**

pledge (plej) *noun*
A solemn promise. She made a *pledge* to help the workers.

Thesaurus
pledge
promise
oath
guarantee

pol·lut·ed
(pə lōō′tid) *verb*
Poisoned the environment with waste. The factory *polluted* the water with chemicals.
▲ **pollute**

proc·ess (pros′es) *noun*
A series of actions that will achieve a purpose.

Thesaurus

process
method
system
procedure

pro•duc•tion
(prə duk′shən) *noun*
The act of making something. The company's methods of *production* were better this year.

pro•pos•al
(prə pō′zəl) *noun*
A plan that is presented to others for their consideration.

raise (rāz) *noun*
An increase in salary.

re•spon•si•ble
(ri spon′sə bəl) *adjective*
In charge of something. She is *responsible* for setting up the chairs.

scab (skab) *noun*
A worker who takes the place of another worker on strike. The striking miners hissed at the *scab*.

seg•re•ga•tion
(seg′ri gā′shən) *noun*
The separation of one group from the rest of society.

Word History

The word **segregation** comes from the Latin word *segregare,* which means "to flock apart."

stand (stand) *noun*
A firm opinion about an issue. He took a *stand* against slavery.

Word Study

The word **stand** can mean:

• to be on your feet; not sitting
• to occupy a place or location
• the place a witness sits to testify in court
• a small open-air place where things are sold

strike (strīk) *verb*
To stop work until certain demands have been met. The union decided to *strike*.

Un•der•ground Rail•road
(un′dər ground′ rāl′rōd′) *noun*
The name of the escape system used by slaves in the South to travel north to freedom.

Fact File

• From the 1840s to the 1860s, the **Underground Railroad** helped 60,000 slaves escape to freedom.

• Harriet Tubman, a famous "conductor," helped over 300 slaves escape to freedom.

un•ion
(yōōn yən) *noun*
A group of workers who join together to improve their working conditions and protect their interests.

zo•ol•o•gist
(zō ol′ə jist) *noun*
A scientist who studies animals.

a	add	ŏŏ	took	ə =
ā	ace	ōō	pool	a in *above*
â	care	u	up	e in *sicken*
ä	palm	û	burn	i in *possible*
e	end	yōō	fuse	o in *melon*
ē	equal	oi	oil	u in *circus*
i	it	ou	pout	
ī	ice	ng	ring	
o	odd	th	thin	
ō	open	ŧh	this	
ô	order	zh	vision	

Authors & Illustrators

Natalie Babbitt *pages 32–39*
When Natalie Babbitt was a girl, she spent much of her time drawing and reading fairy tales and myths. Although this author has done a lot of teaching, she doesn't believe that you can teach someone to write. "Nobody can teach you to write a beautiful sentence," she says. "You've got to learn how to do that by reading."

Peter Golenbock *pages 84–97*
This author loves baseball! His two dogs are named after baseball players and his childhood dream was to be a famous baseball player. When Mr. Golenbock was thirteen, he met Jackie Robinson and got to shake his hand. "Mine disappeared in his," he remembers.

Phillip Hoose *pages 62–73*
Phillip Hoose is a lot like James Ale, the boy in his book *It's Our World, Too!* James tries to get a playground built so children will stay out of the busy street. Mr. Hoose also tries to protect people—and animals. At the Nature Conservancy, he works to identify and protect the homes of endangered species. He has also worked to find good living conditions for people in poor inner-city neighborhoods.

Steven Kellogg *pages 32–39*

Award-winning author/illustrator Steven Kellogg has always loved to draw. As a child, he made up stories for his two younger sisters. He would sit between them and scribble pictures on a big pad of paper as he told a story. He does the same thing today! Only now he doesn't scribble, but spends a lot of time on each image. "I'm constantly rethinking, refining, reworking, rearranging," he says.

"Words and pictures are like two voices, singing different melodies. Together, they blend to make it more meaningful than either voice could be on its own."

Faith Ringgold *pages 10–31*

The family traditions of storytelling and sewing inspired Faith Ringgold in creating her unique form of picture books. Her stories are told on "story quilts" that combine sewing, painting, and storytelling on a patchwork quilt. *Dinner at Aunt Connie's House* is based on her "Dinner Quilt," which has been exhibited at major museums throughout the country.

Lannis Temple *pages 112–113*

Lannis Temple was unhappy being a lawyer, so he decided to do what he loved best: travel. Everywhere he went, he met friendly people. And he saw pollution. He decided to gather together letters and drawings from children all over the world who were also concerned about pollution.

Books &

More by Faith Ringgold

Tar Beach
Faith Ringgold's first picture book is based on her own childhood memories of warm summer nights in the city.

Aunt Harriet's Underground Railroad in the Sky
This book combines great art, historical facts, and a fantasy adventure to create a portrait of Harriet Tubman. She exemplified the courage of all those who traveled on the Underground Railroad.

Harriet Tubman

Jackson Jones and the Puddle of Thorns
by Mary Quattlebaum
illustrated by Melody Rosales
Jackson is hoping to get a new basketball for his birthday. Instead, he gets a plot in a community garden! What does a city boy know about growing flowers?

Oh, Honestly, Angela!
by Nancy K. Robinson
Angela watches as her older sister and brother try to raise money for Rescue the Children. Determined to help out, Angela takes matters into her own hands, with hilarious results.

Is There a Woman in the House... or Senate?
by Bryna J. Fireside
These ten true stories tell about American women who made their mark in politics.

The Scholastic Encyclopedia of the Presidents and Their Times
This book, full of pictures and facts, gives a history of our presidents.

Wanted Dead or Alive: The True Story of Harriet Tubman
by Ann McGovern
This dramatic biography tells the story of the courageous woman who led many slaves to freedom.

xMedia

 Videos

 Software

 Magazines

Videos

And the Children Shall Lead
Public Media Video/ WonderWorks
The year is 1964 and the Civil Rights Movement is just gaining momentum. Twelve-year-old Rachel proves that children can make a difference. (60 minutes)

Brontosaurus
Video Gems
A boy fears that the littered forest near his home will soon become extinct. (70 minutes)

Sadako and the Thousand Paper Cranes
Informed Democracy
Sadako survived the atomic bomb that fell on Hiroshima when she was two, only to develop leukemia at eleven. Her courage inspired an international peace movement. (30 minutes)

Software

Ace Reporter
Mindplay
(Apple, IBM, MAC)
Read teletypes and conduct interviews to gather facts for writing an article.

Instant Survey
MECC
(Apple)
What issues matter to you? Use this program to design and conduct your own surveys on subjects that you find important.

Newsroom
Queue
(Apple, IBM)
Design, produce, and print your own newspaper. A large library of clip art is included to help you illustrate your articles.

Magazines

Scholastic News
Scholastic Inc.
This award-winning publication brings the world to you.

U*S* Kids
Field Publications
This magazine will keep you up-to-date with what is happening all over America.

A Place to Write

Children's Express
30 Cooper Square, 4th floor
New York, NY 10003

Write to this international news service, for and about young people, to find out how you can become a reporter for them.

Acknowledgments

Grateful acknowledgment is made to the following sources for permission to reprint from previously published material. The publisher has made diligent efforts to trace the ownership of all copyrighted material in this volume and believes that all necessary permissions have been secured. If any errors or omissions have inadvertently been made, proper corrections will gladly be made in future editions.

Cover: © Mark Selinger/Outline/Jennifer Hazen 1986.

Interior: "Dinner at Aunt Connie's House" from DINNER AT AUNT CONNIE'S HOUSE by Faith Ringgold. Text and illustrations copyright © 1993 by Faith Ringgold. Reprinted by permission of Hyperion.

"The Last Days of the Giddywit" by Natalie Babbit from THE BIG BOOK FOR OUR PLANET. Text copyright © 1993 by Natalie Babbit. Reprinted by permission of the author. Illustrations copyright © 1993 by Steven Kellogg, first published by E. P. Dutton in THE BIG BOOK FOR OUR PLANET.

"Eye on the Prize" is excerpted from ZuZu Journal, September/October 1993. By permission of Restless Youth Press, 271 E. 10th Street, #64, New York, NY 10009. ZuZu logo used by permission.

Survey from BRIGHT IDEAS: ENVIRONMENTAL STUDIES by Alistair Ross. Copyright © 1988 Scholastic Publications Ltd. "Families and Free Time" bar graph (p. 47) based on graph from Scholastic News, vol. 53, no. 17, February 15, 1985.

Selections and cover from TROUBLE AT THE MINES by Doreen Rappaport. Text copyright © 1987 by Doreen Rappaport. Reprinted by permission of HarperCollins Publishers.

"James Ale" and cover from IT'S OUR WORLD, TOO! by Phillip Hoose. Copyright © 1993 by Phillip Hoose. Reprinted by permission of Little, Brown and Company.

American Red Cross Public Service Announcement used by the kind permission of The American Red Cross.

"Teammates" from TEAMMATES by Peter Golenbock, illustrated by Paul Bacon. Text copyright © 1990 by Golenbock Communications, Inc. Illustrations copyright © 1990 by Paul Bacon. Reprinted by permission of Harcourt Brace and Company.

"Save My Rainforest" from SAVE MY RAINFOREST by Monica Zak, illustrated by Bengt-Arne Runnerström, English version by Nancy Schimmel. Text copyright © 1987 by Monica Zak, English language text copyright © 1992 by Volcano Press, Inc. Originally published in Sweden under the title RÄDDA MIN DJUNGEL by Bokförlaget Opal, 1989. This edition is published by special arrangement with Volcano Press, Inc.

Selections and cover from DEAR WORLD, edited by Lannis Temple. Copyright © 1992 by Lannis Temple. Reprinted by permission of Random House, Inc.

Cover from CLASS PRESIDENT by Johanna Hurwitz, illustrated by John Rosato. Illustration copyright © 1991 by John Rosato. Published by William Morrow & Company, Inc.

Cover from THE GREAT SQUIRREL UPRISING by Dan Elish, illustrated by Denys Cazet. Illustration copyright © 1992 by Denys Cazet. Published by Orchard Books.

Cover from SWEET CLARA AND THE FREEDOM QUILT by Deborah Hopkinson, illustrated by James Ransome. Illustration copyright © 1993 by James Ransome. Published by Alfred A. Knopf, Inc.

Cover from WHERE WAS PATRICK HENRY ON THE 29TH OF MAY? by Jean Fritz, illustrated by Margot Tomes. Illustration copyright © 1975 by Margot Tomes. Published by The Putnam Publishing Group.

Photography and Illustration Credits

Photos: © John Lei for Scholastic Inc., all Tool Box items unless otherwise noted. p. 2 cl: © John Bessler for Scholastic Inc.; bl, tl: © James Lukoski for Scholastic Inc. pp. 2-3 background: © John Lei for Scholastic Inc. p. 3 bc: © James Lukoski for Scholastic Inc.; tc: © Ana Esperanza Nance for Scholastic Inc. pp. 4-6: © Ana Esperanza Nance for Scholastic Inc. pp. 8-9 © Paul Barton/The Stock Market. pp. 40-41 bc: © Henry Garfunkel. pp. 44-45 br: © David S. Waitz for Scholastic Inc. p. 46 bc: © Stanley Bach for Scholastic Inc.; br: © Mike Wilson/FPG Interntional. p. 47 bc: © Stanley Bach for Scholastic Inc.;br:John Lei for Scholastic Inc. pp. 48-49: © The Bettmann Archive. p. 62 bc: © Ana Esperanza Nance for Scholastic Inc. pp. 72-73: © Ana Esperanza Nance for Scholastic Inc. p. 74 cl: © John Lei for Scholastic Inc.; tl, bl: © James Lukoski for Scholastic Inc.; tr: © John Bessler for Scholastic Inc.; tc: © Ana Esperanza Nance for Scholastic Inc. pp. 74-75 c: © John Lei for Scholastic Inc. p. 75 tr: © John Bessler for Scholastic Inc. p. 76 bl: © John Lei for Scholastic Inc.; tr: © John Bessler for Scholastic Inc. p. 77 cr, tr: © John Lei for Scholastic Inc.; bl: © John Bessler for Scholastic Inc. pp. 78-79 bc: © John Lei for Scholastic Inc. p. 80 br: © Stanley Bach for Scholastic Inc.; bl: © John Lei for Scholastic Inc. p. 81 tr: © J. Taposchaner/FPG International. pp. 82-83: © C.C. Lockwood/Earth Scenes. pp. 84-85 tl: © Richard Megna/Fundamental Graphics. pp. 114-115 bc: © John Lei for Scholastic Inc. p. 116 bl, c: © John Lei for Scholastic Inc.; br: © Stanley Bach for Scholastic Inc. p. 117 bl, tl: © John Lei for Scholastic Inc.; br: © Ken Reid/FPG International. tr: © Stanley Bach for Scholastic Inc. p. 118 br: © Joseph Devenney/The Image Bank; bc: © Stanley Bach for Scholastic Inc.; stamps: © John Lei for Scholastic Inc. p. 119 c: © Stanley Bach for Scholastic Inc. p. 121 c: © Robert Reiff/FPG International Corp.; lc: © Errol Andrew/FPG International Corp.; cr: © Larry Grant/FPG International Corp. p. 124 tl: © Avi; cl: © Courtesy of Harcourt Brace; bl: © Little Brown & Company, Boston. p. 125 tr: © Courtesy of Penguin USA; br: © Courtesy of Lannis Temple. p. 126 bl: © Schomburg Center for Research in Black Culture; p. 127 br: © Stephen Ogilvy for Scholastic Inc.

Illustrations: pp. 64, 67, 70: Lyle Miller. pp. 114-115: Jared D. Lee.